THE YUVRAJ SINGH

MR VIVEK KUMAR PANDEY SHAMBHUNATH

Copyright © Mr Vivek Kumar Pandey Shambhunath
All Rights Reserved.

ISBN 978-1-63974-104-5

This book has been published with all efforts taken to make the material error-free after the consent of the author. However, the author and the publisher do not assume and hereby disclaim any liability to any party for any loss, damage, or disruption caused by errors or omissions, whether such errors or omissions result from negligence, accident, or any other cause.

While every effort has been made to avoid any mistake or omission, this publication is being sold on the condition and understanding that neither the author nor the publishers or printers would be liable in any manner to any person by reason of any mistake or omission in this publication or for any action taken or omitted to be taken or advice rendered or accepted on the basis of this work. For any defect in printing or binding the publishers will be liable only to replace the defective copy by another copy of this work then available.

MY NAME IS VIVEK KUMAR PANDEY . I WAS BORN IN 30 SEP 2002,I AM FROM SURAT GUJARAT INDIA.MY DREAM WAS TO BE GOOD WRITERS ,MY FAMILY SUPPORTED ME TO SUCCESSFUL AND I CAN DO IT MY SELF.How do I write? That is a question, I believe, that cannot be honestly answered by me."CELEBRATING YOUNGEST WRITER AWARD WINNER IN GUJARAT 1ST RANK" MR PANDEY JI . I may think I did a good job writing something when in reality it could be horrible. The reader is the one who decides the quality of my writing. I do not find writing to be natural to me and therefore find it to be a real challenge. My trick as a challenged writer is to do the best I can and know that I am happy with the final outcome. It may take a while to do my best and there may be quite a few problems I run into along the way.

I am not a greedy person those who are thinking about me and my self I never tried it anyone people suffering from sadness ,I trying to get promoted people suffering from happiness and joy in your Life Time. Now in current situation in India and also world people are unemployed and have no many but our indian governor help to people to get free food from ration card , i also take part in leadership team ,i am Motivational speaker , Film script writer. There was my two dream firstly writer and secondly actor & also my own film is upcoming soon i done almost completely completed script for my film .I AM GOING TO SAY WORD OF HEART TOUCH OUT PLEASE READ IT" , firstly i thanks my father he supports me in this field they always getting inspired me by own his words and behavior ,they always said that he was a biggest person in the world in future and also they purchase fruit and chocolate for me in anytime & anyway , firstly my father buy him then call me Vivek you want a chocolate i will say yes papa but how many tell me ,papa: you tell me how much i buy him i told 1 or 2 chocolate but my father purchase whole the boxes of chocolate and they get suprised me. MY FATHER WAS BORN IN " 20 SEPTEMBER" 1971 IN INDIA.

1) MY FATHER FAVORITE CLOTHES IS KURTA PAIJMA AND ALSO STYLES SHOE

2) FAVORITE SINGER IS KISHORE DA

3) FAVORITE STATE GUJARAT AND KOLKATA , HIS VILLAGE IN BIHAR

4) FAVORITE COLOR BLACK AND WHITE

THEY ALSO LOVE cricket like IPL and one day t-20 .they also like watching a News daily and heard the song daily ,they also interested in tik tok video but in current time tik tok is banned in india but also few videos are in you tube. In lockdown time my family and me very enjoy day daily. my father play daily ludo with his sister and son, daughter.they always loved tea and coffee anytime call me "। विवेक थोडा़ चाय बनाओना विवेक तुम्हारे हाथ का चाय अच्छा लगता है". I make it tea for my father but some reason after the April to june they are suffering from fever and cough , weakness on 6 June 2020 my father death. they not told me say bye bye his life. After death of 6 June on 10 june my mom and dad anniversary.but my father is Best in the world they can do anything for me please take care of father and respect it of your parents

Contents

Foreword — vii
Preface — ix

   1. The Yuvraj Singh — 1

Foreword

Short biography of yuvraj singh and about life ,during writing this book no character & no religious are harmed written by mr vivek kumar pandey. winner youngest writer award 1st rank in india 2020.He is only one writer can publish 600+ own book that was greatest successfull in his life.

Preface

Yuvraj Singh

Yuvraj Singh(born 12 December 1981) is a former Indian international cricketer who played in all formats of the game. An all-rounder who bats left-handed in the middle order and bowls slow left-arm orthodox, Yuvraj is the son of former Indian fast bowler and Punjabi actor Yograj Singh. One of the greatest limited over players to play for India, Yuvraj was particularly noted for his aggressive stroke play of the ball and his fielding.

CHAPTER ONE

The Yuvraj Singh

Yuvraj Singh

Yuvraj Singh(born 12 December 1981) is a former Indian international cricketerwho played in all formats of the game. An all-rounder who bats left-handed in the middle order and bowls slow left-arm orthodox, Yuvraj is the son of former Indian fast bowler and Punjabi actor Yograj Singh. One of the greatest limited over players to play for India, Yuvraj was particularly noted for his aggressive stroke play of the ball and his fielding.

Yuvraj was a member of the Indian cricket team in One Day Internationals (ODIs) between 2000 and 2017 and played his first Test match in October 2003. He was the vice-captain of the Indian ODI team between 2007 and 2008. He was the Man of the Tournament in the 2011 ICC Cricket World Cup, and one of the top performers at the 2007 ICC World T20, both of which India won. In a match against Englandat the 2007 World T20, he famously hit six sixesin one over bowled by Stuart Broad— a feat performed only three times previously in any form of senior cricket, and never in an international match between two teams with Test match status. In the same match, he set the record for the fastest fifty in Twenty20 Internationals and in all T20 cricket, reaching 50 runs in 12 balls. During the 2011 World Cup, he became the first player to take a 5-wicket haul and score a 50 in the same World Cupmatch.

In 2011, Yuvraj was diagnosed with a canceroustumorin his left lung and underwent chemotherapytreatment in Boston and Indianapolis.In March 2012, he was discharged from the hospital after completing the third and final cycle of chemotherapy and returned to India in April. He made his international comeback in a Twenty20 match in September against New Zealand shortly before the 2012 World Twenty20.

In 2012, Yuvraj was conferred with the Arjuna Award, India's second highest sporting award by the Government of India. In 2014, he was awarded the Padma Shri, India's fourth highest civilian honour. At the 2014 IPL auction Royal Challengers Bangalore bought Yuvraj for an all-time high price of 14 crore and, in 2015, the Delhi Daredevils bought him for 16 crore making him the second most expensive player ever to be sold in the IPL until Chris Morris was sold to the Rajasthan Royals for a record 16.25 crore in February 2021. In February 2014, he was honoured with FICCI Most Inspiring Sportsperson of the Year Award.

On 10 June 2019, Yuvraj announced his retirement from all forms of International cricket. He last represented India in June 2017, against the West Indies.[7] His request for a return to domestic cricket and IPL was turned down by BCCI for participating in Global T20 League in Canada and T10 league.

Early years and personal life

Singh was born in a Punjabi Sikh family to Yograj Singh, a former India cricketer, and Shabnam Singh. Tennis and roller skating were Yuvraj's favourite sports during his childhood and he was quite good at both. He had also won the National Under-14 Roller Skating Championship. His father threw away the medal and told him to forget skating and concentrate on cricket. He would take Yuvraj to training every day.

Yuvraj studied at the DAV Public School in Chandigarh. He completed his graduation degree in Commerce from DAV College, Panjab University, Chandigarh.[12] He also did two short roles as child star in *Mehndi Sagna Di and Putt Sardara.*

In 2015, Yuvraj got engaged to Hazel Keech and married her in November 2016.[13] In February 2021, he purchased a luxury penthouse in Chattarpur, South Delhi.

Career

Youth career

Yuvraj began his career with Punjab Under-16s at the age of 13 years and 11 months in November of the 1995-96 season against Jammu and Kashmir-16s. In 1996-97, Yuvraj was promoted to Punjab Under-19s and scored 137 not out against Himachal Pradesh Under-19s.

Yuvraj made his first-class debut in late-1997 against Orissa during the 1997-98 Ranji Trophy but was dismissed for a duck opening the innings. His first break-out performance came in the Under-19 Cooch Behar Trophy Final of 1999 against Bihar at Jamshedpur; Bihar were all out with a score of 357 and Yuvraj batted at three for Punjab and made 358 runs himself.[18] Yuvraj represented India in the series against Sri Lanka Under-19s in India in February 1999. In the third ODI, Yuvraj scored 89 runs from 55 balls.[19] In 1999-2000 Ranji Trophy, he scored 149 against Haryana.

In the 2000 Under-19 Cricket World Cup which India won under the captaincy of Mohammad Kaif, Yuvraj's all-round performance earned him the Player of the Tournament award and a call-up to the national squad. His performance in the tournament included 68 off 62 and 4/36 against New Zealand in a group stage match,[21] and a quickfire 58 off 25 balls against Australia in the semifinal.[22] Yuvraj was subsequently selected in 2000 for the first intake of cricketers in the National Cricket Academy in Bangalore.

International breakthrough

Yuvraj was selected in the Indian squad for the 2000 ICC KnockOut Trophy on the back of his impressive performances for the Under-19 team. He made his international debut against Kenya in the pre-quarterfinal. He bowled four overs conceding 16 runs but did not get to bat. In the quarterfinal match against Australia, Yuvraj won the man of the match for his innings of 84 out of 80 balls, against a pace attack consisting of Glenn McGrath, Brett Lee and Jason Gillespie, that helped India win by 20 runs.[24] In the semifinal against South Africa, he scored 41 and picked 1/15.[25] He scored only 14 against New Zealand in the final which India lost. The tournament was followed by a tri-series involving India, Sri

Lanka and Zimbabwe. Yuvraj scored just 55 runs in five innings at an average of 11. Yuvraj averaged 15.50 in the ODI series against the touring Zimbabwe side in December 2000 after which he was dropped from the team.

Yuvraj made his comeback during the 2001 Coca-Cola Cup in Sri Lanka. He scored a crucial 98* against Sri Lankain the fifth match of an otherwise disappointing series with the bat.[26] However, he proved to be useful with the ball as he took 8 wickets at an average of 27.[27] In the Standard Bank triangular series involving hosts South Africa, India and Kenya, Yuvraj managed to score only 69 runs from 6 innings, including a duck in the final against South Africa.[28] Following this, Dinesh Mongiaand Hemang Badaniwere chosen over Yuvraj in the squad for the home series against England in January 2002.

Yuvraj returned to domestic cricket in early 2002. After a disappointing run in the Ranji knockouts, Yuvraj struck 209 for North Zoneagainst South Zonein a Duleep Trophymatch in March 2002.[29] He was immediately drafted into the national squad for the final two ODIs against Zimbabwewith India trailing the series 1–2. Yuvraj made an impact in his return match at Hyderabad, scoring an unbeaten 80 off just 60 balls, taking India to a five-wicket win and levelling the series. He won the Man of the Match award for his efforts.[30] In the final ODI at Guwahati, Yuvraj made 75 runs from 52 balls, sharing a 157-run fifth-wicket partnership with Mongia who scored his career-best unbeaten 159, to help India post a total of 333 in their 50 overs. India went on to win the game by 101 runs and the series 3–2.[31]

2002 NatWest Series

After winning the ODI series in the West Indies 2–1, where Yuvraj managed scores of only 1 and 10, the Indian team toured England in June for the NatWest triangular series, featuring England, Sri Lanka, and India, and a four-match Test series against the hosts. In the first match at Lord's, Yuvraj won the man of the match for his all-round performance (3/39 and 64*) as India successfully chased down England's total of 271.[32] In the next match against Sri Lanka, he scored 31 and shared a crucial 60-run sixth-wicket partnership with Mohammad Kaif to set up another successful run-chase.[33] India's next match against England was washed out due to rain after Yuvraj had scored an unbeaten 40 off 19 balls to take India to 285/4 in their 50 overs.[34] Yuvraj's knock of 37, along with a fifty from Rahul Dravid, helped India recover from 59/4 to reach a target of 188 posted by Sri Lanka.[35] This win eliminated Sri Lanka from the series with another round of matches still to be played. Yuvraj had scores of 5 and 8 in the final round of matches but proved to be useful with the ball as he picked one wicket in each of the two games. At the end of the round-robin matches, India topped the points table with 19 points while England finished second with 15 points.[36]

The final was played at Lord's on 13 July between India and England. After winning the toss and electing to bat first, England posted a daunting total of 325/5 in 50 overs. In reply, India was struggling at 146/5 at the end of 24 overs, when Kaif joined Yuvraj at the crease. The pair initially stabilised the innings and later scored at a brisk rate. The pair shared a partnership of 121 runs for the sixth wicket which came to an end when Yuvraj was dismissed for 69 off 63 balls when he top-edged a sweep shot in the 42nd over off the bowling of Paul Collingwood resulting in a simple catch to Alex Tudor at short fine leg. India went on to win the game by two wickets with three balls to spare.[37] This was India's first win in the final of an ODI tournament since 2000, after nine consecutive defeats.[38] This win is regarded as one of India's greatest victories in ODI cricket.[39]

Highs and lows

Yuvraj batted in two games of the 2002 ICC Champions Trophy which was held in Sri Lanka in September. He scored 3 against Zimbabwe in the opening match, and 62 in the semifinal against South Africa. In November 2002, Yuvraj struggled in the first five games of the 7-match ODI series against West Indies, with a high score of 30. He returned to form in the sixth ODI at Jodhpur with a half-century that helped India win the match by three wickets and level the series 3-3.[40] He top-scored for India in the 7th match with a 69-ball 68, but could not get support from any other batsman. India crashed to a 135-run defeat and lost the series.[41] He struggled for runs in the seven-match ODI series in New Zealand in December 2002-January 2003, averaging just above 19 with a solitary fifty.

Despite his average form leading up to the 2003 ICC Cricket World Cup in South Africa, Yuvraj secured a place in the 15-man Indian squad for the tournament. He scored 37 in India's opening match against Netherlands. In the following games, he had scores of 0, 1 and 7* against Australia, Zimbabwe and Namibia respectively. He then scored a brisk 42 against England, followed by an unbeaten 50 against Pakistan setting up wins for India in both games. In the Super Six stage of the tournament, Yuvraj had scores of 58* against Kenya and 5 against Sri Lanka. He scored 16 in the semifinal against Kenya, and 24 against Australia in the final.

Yuvraj scored his maiden ODI century (102* from 85 balls) against Bangladesh at Dhaka on 11 April 2003. In May 2003, Yuvraj was signed-up by the Yorkshire County Cricket Club for the 2003 county season. He became only the second Indian after Sachin Tendulkar to represent the county.[42][43] Yuvraj's Test debut came on 16 October 2003 at his home ground Mohali against New Zealand. Batting at six, he scored 20 in the first innings, and 5* in the second innings. In the TVS Cup tri-series in October–November 2003 involving India, Australia and New Zealand, he scored 113 runs from 7 games at an average of 18.83 and top-score of 44.[44]

Yuvraj returned to form in early-2004 in the tri-series involving Australia and Zimbabwe. He scored 314 runs from 8 innings at an average of 39.25, including his second ODI hundred - 139 runs from 122 balls, with 16 fours and two sixes - against Australia at the Sydney Cricket Ground.[45] He had a mixed tour of Pakistan in March–April 2004. He disappointed in the ODI series with 141 runs from 5 matches, averaging just over 28, but found success in the Test series. In the first Test at Multan, he scored 59 - his maiden Test fifty - as India registered an innings win. He also picked his maiden Test wicket during Pakistan's second innings.[46]In the second Test at Lahore, Yuvraj scored his maiden Test century during India's first innings while the rest of the batting line-up struggled against the bowling of Umar Gul. Yuvraj's score of 112 came from just 129 deliveries with 15 fours and two sixes. He made only 12 runs in the second Test as Pakistan levelled the series after winning the match by 9 wickets.[47]He scored 47 in the final Test at Rawalpindiwhere India secured the series with another innings victory.[48]However, he suffered a drop in form in the latter half of 2004 with batting averages of 31 in the 2004 Asia Cup, 12.33 in the Natwest Series in England and just 4.50 in the 2004 ICC Champions Trophy. In October 2004, after the first two Tests of the Border-Gavaskar Trophy, he was dropped from the Test squad as his dismal run with the bat yielded just 47 runs from the two matches.

Despite Yuvraj's loss in form, he continued to be a regular feature in the Indian ODI team. In the Platinum Jubilee Match against Pakistan in November 2004, he scored a 62-ball 78 in a losing cause.[49]In December 2004, Yuvraj scored 94 runs at an average of 31.33 in the three-match ODI tour of Bangladesh including a quickfire knock of 69 from 32 balls in the final ODI at Dhaka.[50]He had a disappointing ODI series at home against Pakistan in April 2005, scoring 98 runs in six matches at 19.60.[51]

Return to form

In July–August 2005, Yuvraj was the leading run-scorer for India in the 2005 Indian Oil Cuptriangular series in Sri Lanka also involving the hosts Sri Lanka and West Indies. He scored 192 runs in four matches, averaging 48.[52]He also recorded his third ODI century during the series - 110 runs from 114 balls - against the West Indies at Colombofor which he was adjudged the man of the match.[53]Yuvraj then played in the Videocon Cupin August–September 2005, a triangular series involving India, New Zealand and the hosts Zimbabwe. He averaged 54 with the bat in the series, scoring 216 runs from 5 matches.[54]He scored 120 in the final round-robin match against Zimbabwe at Harare, helping India recover from 36/4 to successfully chase down a target of 251. It was his fourth ODI hundred and he won the man of the match award for his efforts.[55] In the two-match Test tour of Zimbabwe that followed the tri-series, Yuvraj scored 12 and 25 runs. In October–November 2005, Yuvraj had a quiet seven-match ODI series at home against Sri Lanka. He managed just 124 runs in six innings at an average of 31 with a top-score of 79*.

In November 2005, Yuvraj scored 103 in the first ODI against South Africa at Hyderabad to take India from 35/5 to a respectable total of 249/9, and won the man of the match award despite South Africa winning the game by five wickets.[56] He picked 1/17 and remained not out in the second ODI at Bangalore, before the third match at Chennai was washed out due to rain. He scored 53 and 49 in the final two matches at Delhi and Ahmedabad respectively, and the series was drawn 2–2. Yuvraj and South African captain Graeme Smith were jointly awarded the man of the series award as both of them scored 209 runs at 69.66, finishing as the joint-highest run-scorers of the series.[57] Yuvraj had a mixed home Test series against Sri Lanka in December 2005 as he registered two ducks and two half-centuries. He scored 0 & 77* in the second Test at Delhi, and 0 & 75 in the third Test at Ahmedabad as India won both the matches by comfortable margins.

Yuvraj was picked in both Test and ODI squads for the Pakistan tour in January–February 2006. The first two Tests were drawn and Yuvraj batted only once, in the second Test, scoring 4. In the third Test at Karachi, he top-scored for India in both innings. After scoring 45 in the first innings, he went to score his second Test hundred in the second innings (122 runs from 144 balls). India lost the match by 341 runs and the series 1–0.[58] In the one-day series, he continued his good form. He scored a 28-ball 39 in the first ODI at Peshawar which Pakistan won by 7 runs by the Duckworth–Lewis method.[59] He scored an unbeaten 82 in the second match at Rawalpindi taking India to an emphatic 7-wicket win,[60] before scoring an unbeaten 79 in the third game at Lahore and helping India successfully chase the target of 289.[61] In the low-scoring fourth match at Multan, he scored 37 as India took the series with a five-wicket victory.[62] In the fifth and the final ODI at Karachi, Yuvraj, batting at three, hit his sixth ODI century. His innings of 107* which came off 93 balls with 13 boundaries helped India comfortably chase down a target of 287 while losing only two wickets. He won the man of the match award for this innings and was also adjudged player of the series.[63]

Against England, Yuvraj averaged 21.33 in two Tests in March but proved to be successful with both bat and ball in the ODI series in which he again won the player of the series award. During the series, he won the back-to-back man of the match awards in the third and fourth ODIs. In the third match, he made 103 from 76 balls, and in the fourth match, he picked 2/34 and scored 48. He scored a total of 237 runs in the series at an average of 47.40 and took 6 wickets with his part-time bowling.[64]

On India's tour of the West Indies, Yuvraj hit two fifties in the ODI series. In the second ODI at Kingston, with India needing two runs to win with one wicket in hand and three balls to spare, Yuvraj was bowled by Dwayne Bravo for 93. India went on to lose the series 4–1. His poor run of form in Tests continued, with him scoring 104 runs from four matches at an average of 17.33 and a top-score of 39. In September 2006, Yuvraj was dropped from the playing eleven during the 2006-07 DLF Cup in Kuala Lumpur after he registered two consecutive ducks against Australia and West Indies. He played in two group matches of the 2006 ICC Champions Trophy held in India in October. and scored 27* against England and 27 against West Indies. During a training session before India's final group fixture against Australia, Yuvraj suffered a ligament injury in his left knee. Dinesh Mongia replaced him for the match which India lost to crash out of the tournament. In November, Indian team physio Andrew Leipus suggested that Yuvraj was unlikely to recover from the injury before the start of the World Cup in March 2007.[65]

Yuvraj was not named in any of the Indian squads that toured South Africa in late 2006. In January 2007, less than two months before the World Cup, he made a comeback from injury for the last two matches of the four-match ODI series against West Indies, but did not make much of an impact in either game. Despite concerns over his fitness, Yuvraj was selected in the 15-man Indian squad for the 2007 Cricket World Cup, with chief selector Dilip Vengsarkarconfirming that Yuvraj was fit.[66]He featured in the last two matches of the four-ODI seriesagainst Sri Lanka in February 2007, and struck an unbeaten 83-ball 95 in the deciding final game at Visakhapatnam. India won the match by seven wickets and the series 2–1.[67]

Yuvraj made 47 in India's first match of the World Cup, a shock defeat to Bangladesh.[68]In India's next group match at Port-of-Spain against World Cup debutants Bermuda, he hit 83 off 46 balls to help India post a total of 413/5, the highest total in World Cup history at the time.[69]After their emphatic against Bermuda, India were left with a must-win final group fixture against Sri Lanka. Chasing 255 to win the match, Yuvraj was run outfor 6, as India were bowled out for 185 and made an early exit from the World Cup.

In the three-match ODI seriesagainst South Africa in Ireland, Yuvraj took 3 for 36 and scored an unbeaten 49 in the second ODI[70]before winning man of the match for his unbeaten 61 in the series-deciding final game.[71]On India's tour of England, Yuvraj remained on the bench throughout the Test series before finishing third on the run-scorers list in the ODI series with 283 runs from 7 matches at an average of 40.42.[72]

2007 World Twenty20 and vice-captaincy

Yuvraj was the vice-captain of the Indian squad at the inaugural ICC World Twenty20in South Africa. In India's Super 8 match against England at Durban, he hit six sixesin an over off Stuart Broad. In the process, he reached the fastest fifty ever in a Twenty20game, off just 12 balls, which was also the fastest in any form of international cricket.[73][74][75]This was the fourth time that six sixes had been hit in one over in senior cricket, the first time in Twenty20 cricket, and the first time in any form of international cricket against a bowler from a Test playing nation. He finished his innings with 58 runs off 16 balls and won the man of the match.

Yuvraj missed the next game against South Africa due to a minor [76]but recovered before the semifinal against Australia. In the semifinal, he top-scored with 70 off 30 balls and also hit the longest six of the tournament (119 metres (390 ft)) off the bowling of Brett Lee).[77]The knock later was named the Best Twenty20 Batting Performance of 2007 by ESPN Cricinfo.[78]India won the match as Yuvraj was awarded another man of the match award.[79]He was dismissed for 14 in the final against Pakistan but India went on to win by five runs and win the tournament. All players of the victorious Indian team were given a cash reward of ?80 lakh by the BCCI while Yuvraj was rewarded with an additional ?1 crore as well as a Porsche 911by the BCCI vice-president Lalit Modi.[80]He was named in the 'Team of the Tournament' by Cricinfo for the 2007 T20I World Cup.[81]

In September 2007, Mahendra Singh Dhoniand Yuvraj were named ODI captain and vice-captain respectively, following the resignation of Rahul Dravid. Yuvraj scored 121 at Hyderabad in a losing cause in the third of the seven ODIs against Australia, but accumulated only 71 in the other six matches of the series.[82]He enjoyed a return to form in India's home ODI series against Pakistanin November 2007. He scored four half-centuries in five matches, averaging 68,[83]and was named player of the series as India won the series 3–2. He was also fined for showing dissent in the final match in Jaipur. Although Yuvraj was included in Indian squad for the subsequent Test series against Pakistan, Test captain Anil Kumblesaid that Yuvraj "will have to wait a little bit more to become a regular member in the Test squad."[84]He did not feature in the playing eleven in the first two matches, but was picked in the third Test at Bangalore to replace an injured Sachin Tendulkar. Batting first, India was 61/4 before Yuvraj and Sourav Ganguly[85]shared a 300-run fifth-wicket partnership, and Yuvraj recorded his highest Test score of 169 off 203 balls,[86]while Ganguly went on to score 239 which was also his highest score in tests.

For his performances in 2007, he was named in the World ODI XI by Cricinfo.[87] He was also named in the World T20I XI by Cricinfo.[87]

Yuvraj had a poor Test series against Australia in Indian tour to that country in 2007/08. After his poor showing in the first two Tests, he was dropped for the remainder of the series. In November 2008, he hit 138 not out from 78 balls against England at Rajkot, taking 64 balls to reach his century which at the time was the second fastest by an Indian in ODIs after Mohammad Azharuddin's century in 1988 against New Zealand came off 62 balls. After reaching 50 from 42 balls, he added an additional 88 runs in the next 36 balls. He did so despite straining his back, which necessitated the use of Gautam Gambhir as a runner. This was followed by a score of 118 off 122 balls and bowling figures of 4/28, with all of his wickets being specialist batsmen, in the next match in Indore, earning him two consecutive man of the match awards. Yuvraj scored 85 not out and put on an unbroken partnership of 163 with Sachin Tendulkar to defeat England in the First Test at Chennai in December 2008. It was the fourth highest successful run chase in history and the highest in India. Yuvraj scored a quick, unbeaten 54 in the second innings of the Napier Test against New Zealand to help India save the game after following on. India preserved their series lead and went on to win the series 1–0.

For his performances in 2008, he was named in the World ODI XI by the Cricinfo.[88]

For his performances in 2009, he was named in the World ODI XI by the ICC.[89]

Yuvraj was dropped from the Asia Cup following the team's return from the World Twenty20 in West Indies. A drop in form, disciplinary issues and fitness were talked of as the reasons for his exclusion, but he made a return for the series against Sri Lanka. With Suresh Raina scoring a century on Test debut and Cheteshwar Pujara making a compelling case for higher honours with consistent first-class performances, Yuvraj was dropped from the Test squad for the two-match series against Australia.

Golden World Cup

Yuvraj had a dream run at the 2011 ICC Cricket World Cup, where he scored 362 runs including one century and four fifties, took 15 wickets, won four Man of the Match awards, the joint-most along with Sri Lanka's Aravinda de Silva in 1996 and South Africa's Lance Klusener in 1999, and was also adjudged the Player of the Tournament. In the process, he became the first allrounder to score 300-plus runs and take 15 wickets in a single World Cup. In India's match against Ireland, he became the first player to take 5 Wickets and score 50 runs in a World Cup match. He also took his 100th ODI wicket with the dismissal of Wesley Barresi in the World Cup match against the Netherlands. He later took 2/44 and scored 57 runs against defending champions Australia in the quarter finals, earning him the Man of the Match award.

Yuvraj had respiratory difficulties through 2011 and in May he withdrew from the ODI series in the West Indies due to an illness. His issues began with breathing difficulties, nausea and bouts of vomiting blood. He toured England but had to return home after breaking his finger in the Nottingham Test and later played two home Tests against West Indies. However, he then pulled out of the ODI series against West Indies in November citing an abnormal tumor in his lung. Yuvraj had originally targeted the CB series in Australia for his return to international cricket.

After the World Cup he was diagnosed with a cancerous tumor stage-1 in his left lung and underwent chemotherapy treatment at the Cancer Research Institute in Boston, United States as well as the Indiana University Melvin & Bren Simon Cancer Center in Indianapolis, Indiana where he was cared for by famed oncologist Dr. Lawrence Einhorn.

For his performances in 2011, he was named in the World ODI XI by the ICC and Cricinfo. He was named in the 'Team of the Tournament' for the 2011 World Cup by the ICC and Cricinfo.

Cancer diagnosis and comeback

Yuvraj's cancer was detected by a Russian doctor in 2011.[94] In March 2012, Yuvraj was discharged from hospital after completing the third and final cycle of chemotherapy and returned to India in April. After his chemotherapy sessions treating seminomain Indianapolis, Yuvraj's cancer showing full signs of remission, and he aimed at resuming cricket at the World Twenty20. The selectors picked Yuvraj to be a part of the 15-member Indian squad for the 2012 ICC World Twenty20in Sri Lanka in September 2012.

He played against New Zealand in a T20I at Chennaiwhere he scored 34 off 26 balls (1 four, 2 sixes) as his side lost by only 1 run. He started his World Twenty20campaign with a 3/24 against Afghanistan. He took 1/16 against Australia, 2/16 against Pakistan and a 2/23 against South Africa. He ended up being the highest wicket taker for India in the tournament though he could not meet expectations with his bat.

He got selected for the Test series against England at home. He later played 3 test matches in the 4 match test series against England after which he was dropped. He later was selected for the India-Pakistan Series, returning to form in the second T20I by scoring a blistering 72 off just 36 balls. He could not make an impact in the One Day series against Pakistan and England, only scoring 1 half century in 7 matches.

For his performances in 2012, he was named in the T20I XI of the year by Cricinfo.[95]

In September 2013, Yuvraj made a comeback to India's limited-overs squad for the Twenty20 and first three ODIs of the home series against Australia.

In October 2013, Yuvraj scored 77 off 35 in the only T20I against Australia at Saurashtra Cricket Association Stadiumin Rajkot. India faced a required run rate of nearly 12 per over when at 100 for 4 in the 12th over, but Yuvraj's unbeaten 102 run partnership with Dhoni guided India to victory.[96]However, Yuvraj had a woeful time in the ODI series that followed, scoring 19 runs in four innings, and being visibly troubled by the pace of Mitchell Johnson.

Yuvraj was unable to return to form in both the home ODIs against West Indiesand in the subsequent tour of South Africa, and was dropped for the New Zealand tour given the conditions in that country and the hosts' pace-heavy attack. He was not selected for 2014 Asia Cup in Bangladesh but he was selected for the 2014 ICC World Twenty20 in the same place. In a Super 10 match against Pakistan he missed a full delivery and was bowled on his second ball by pacer Bilawal Bhatti. In the same match he dropped a catch that would have resulted in the wicket of Mohammad Hafeez, and later against the West Indies dropped a delivery hit by Chris Gayle.

Yuvraj then scored 60 off 43 balls against Australia at Mirpur, his eighth T20I fifty and third against Australia. His 84-run partnership with Mahendra Singh Dhoni is India's third-highest for the fifth wicket.

On 5 July 2014, he played for the Rest of the World XI against the Marylebone Cricket Club (MCC) in the Bicentenary Celebration match at Lord's, as he had been left out of India's ODI team. Under Shane Warne's captaincy, he struck a century at nearly a run a ball to rescue his team, who were struggling at 59 for 3. His 100 came up as he hit Sachin Tendulkar for a boundary. The Rest of the World finished on 293 for 7 after 50 overs, but the MCC went on to win the match by 7 wickets.[97]

Yuvraj in an interview with Hindustan Times during his cancer treatment, said 'Even if I die let India win World Cup'.[98]

Notably, Singh was one of five senior members of India's 2011 World Cup squad who were not considered for the 2015 Cricket World Cup and was not included in India's 30-man probable list for the tournament.[99]

Late career

Singh was picked in India's T20I squad for the January 2016 Australia tour on the back of strong performances in Vijay Hazare Trophy, where he was the third-highest run scorer with 341 runs at an average of 85.25. He finished the three-match series with 15 runs after getting to bat in just one innings, while also taking two wickets. He played a crucial role in India's titular run in Asia Cup 2016, often teaming up with Virat Kohli to take the team home. He was also a part of the Indian team in the ICC T20 World Cup

2016. He was not named in the T20I squad for India's tour of West Indies in August.[100] Meanwhile, he was named captain of the India Red side for the 2016–17 Duleep Trophy. His team lost to India Blue in the final.[101]

Yuvraj was picked in India's ODI squad for the home series against England in January 2017. This came on the back of his fine performances in the Ranji Trophy, having scored 672 runs in five games for Punjab, which included a 260 against Baroda.[102] In the second match of the series, he scored his career best score 150, which came off 127 balls, a knock that included 21 fours and three sixes. He put on 256 runs for the fourth wicket along with Dhoni and helped the team post a total of 381. Following the team's 15-run victory, he was named the Player of the Match.[103]

Following the match, Singh revealed that he had thought of quitting after having been dropped from the team. He said, "When I came back from cancer it was hard work. I was not performing and after being dropped I thought [about] whether I wanted to continue or not."[104]

Yuvraj was selected to play in the Champions Trophy 2017. He scored 53 off 32 balls in a group stage match against Pakistan and won the man of the match award. However, as a result of failing to clear the yo-yo test, Yuvraj was dropped from the squad before the tour of Sri Lanka in August 2017 which ended his international career.

Retirement from international cricket

On 10 June 2019, Yuvraj Singh announced his retirement from international cricket. Yuvraj Singh held a press conference in Mumbai where he announced his decision to retire from all formats of the game. He said that he had decided to "Move On".[105] Yuvraj recounted his best memories through his career, while also recalling his worst.

"I would say I am extremely lucky to play 400-plus games for India. I would've not imagined doing this when I started my career in cricket. Through this journey, some matches that remain in my memory are - the 2002 NatWest series final, my first Test hundred in Lahore in 2004, the 2007 Test series in England, of course the six sixes and the 2007 T20 World Cup. And then the most memorable one was the 2011 World Cup finals."

"And then, probably the worst day in my career, was the 2014 World T20 final against Lanka where I scored 11 off 21 balls. It was so shattering that I felt my career was over."[106]

He also said "As for now, I have decided to provide service and help for cancer affected people."

In September 2020, Yuvraj Singh hinted at making a return to the Punjab team and play domestic T20s for them. He said that it was on the suggestion of Punjab Cricket Association secretary Puneet Bali that he has considered to come out of retirement.[107] However, his return was denied from Punjab Cricket Association, as he took part in foreign franchise league's.[108]

T20 franchise cricket

Indian Premier League

Yuvraj was the icon player and captain for Indian Premier League (IPL) team Kings XI Punjab in the first two seasons; in 2010, the third season, icon player status was discontinued and the captaincy given to Kumar Sangakkara. The Kings XI Punjab came second in the round-robin phase of the tournament, but lost the semi-finals to the Chennai Super Kings. On 1 May 2009, Yuvraj registered his first hat-trick in T20 cricket against Royal Challengers Bangalore at Kingsmead in Durban, the same ground where he hit his six sixes. He dismissed Robin Uthappa, Mark Boucher and Jacques Kallis. On 17 May 2009, Yuvraj took his second Twenty20 hat-trick against Deccan Chargers at the Wanderers Stadium in Johannesburg. Yuvraj dismissed Herschelle Gibbs, Andrew Symonds and Venugopal Rao.

The Pune Warriors were a new team introduced for the 2011 IPL. Yuvraj Singh was bought by the team and chosen as captain.[109] Pune Warriors finished ninth, ahead of only the Delhi Daredevils.[110] From 14 matches, Yuvraj took 11 wickets and also scored 343 runs at an average of 34.30, including two half-centuries.[111] After much controversy, the BCCI allowed Pune

Warriors to find a replacement for Yuvraj for the 2012 Indian Premier League, citing his medical condition and non-availability for 2012 IPL as the reasons for doing so.[112]

In 2014, Yuvraj was bought by the Royal Challengers Bangalorefor 14 crore.[113][114]A Kingfisher employee union sent a letter to Yuvraj requesting him not to play for Royal Challengers Bangalore. He had a successful stint with RCB, scoring 376 runs and taking six wickets. In 2015, he was bought by Delhi Daredevilsfor Rs.16 Crores, the highest ever bid at an IPL auction. at the time.[115][116]

In the 2016 IPL auctionhe was bought by Sunrisers Hyderabadfor Rs.7 crores. He had a very successful IPL campaign with the Sunrisers Hyderabadwith them winning the 2016 Indian Premier League. He played several crucial knocks at crunch moments, and some experts called him the "Unsung hero of SRH's titular run". Yuvraj scored 38 runs from 23 balls in the final.[117]

Yuvraj was retained by Sunrisers Hyderabad for the 2017 Indian Premier League.

In the 2018 IPL auction, he was picked by Kings XI Punjabfor base price of 2 crores. He scored only 64 runs from 6 innings at a low average of 12.80. He batted at four different positions during those six innings and was not given a consistent run by the team management.

Yuvraj was released by Kings XI Punjab ahead of the 2019 IPL Auction, where was purchased by Mumbai Indiansfor his base price of ?1 crore. He scored 53 in his debut match for Mumbai Indians, and smashed a hattrick of sixes against Yuzvendra Chahal in the next match, but he wasn't given a longer run by the team management, and was dropped after he failed in the next two matches.[118]He was released by the Mumbai Indians ahead of the 2020 IPL auction.[119]

Other leagues[edit]

In June 2019, Yuvraj was selected to play for the Toronto Nationals franchise team in the 2019 Global T20 Canadatournament.[120]He also played for the Maratha Arabians in the Abu Dhabi T10 League 2019. In 2020, Yuvraj played in the Ultimate Kricket Challenge.[121]

Playing style

Yuvraj is primarily a left-handed batsmanbut can bowlpart-time left-arm orthodox spin, which he improved in the latter part of his career. He is regarded as a better batsman against fast bowling than spin bowling, and cites the Indian Oil Cup 2005as a turning point in his career.[122]Yuvraj is one of the athletic fielders in the Indian team, fielding primarily at point& covers with a good aim at the stumps. Yuvraj is a natural stroke player with an aggressive style of play, as seen by his strike rate of above 150 in T20 internationals & just below 90 in ODIs. Many regard him as one of the best clean strikers of the ball, with his trademark punch through the covers a treat to watch. When in good touch, he can clear the ropes quite effortlessly. A Cricinforeport published in late 2005 showed that since 1999, he was the fourth most prolific fielder in affecting ODIrun outs, and of those on the list of prolific fielders, he had the second highest rate of effecting a run out.

Achievements and honours

In a 2007 ICC World Twenty20match, he hit six sixesin a single over.

- He holds the record for fastest T20 fifty by scoring it in 12 balls against England national cricket teamduring the 2007 ICC World Twenty20
- He was the Man of the Tournament in the ICC Cricket World Cup 2011.
- He was awarded with the Arjuna Award(India's second highest, Sporting Award) in 2012 by the President of India.
- In 2014, he was awarded with the Padma Shri Award.
- In February 2014, he was honoured with FICCIMost Inspiring Sportsperson of the Year Award.[125]

Outside cricket
Charity and commercial interests

Yuvraj was signed by Microsoft to be a brand ambassador for the Xbox 360 video game console when it was launched in India in 2006. He appeared in advertisements for the console alongside Bollywood actor Akshay Kumar. Codemasters' cricket video game *Brian Lara International Cricket 2007* was released with his endorsement in India, titled "Yuvraj Singh International Cricket 2007".[126] The Bollywood animated film, Jumbo features cricketer Yuvraj Singh's voice therefore starting his career in Bollywood.[127] The upcoming animated full-length feature film *Captain India* features Yuvraj Singh as the main protagonist.[128]

Yuvraj has also been involved in sports based e-commerce; he is a brand ambassador of sports365.in, an online store focused on selling sports goods and fitness equipment. Yuvraj is also the brand ambassador for the sports brand Puma.[129] He was appointed as the brand ambassador of Ulysse Nardin watch in 2013.

Yuvraj's own charity YouWeCan has treated over hundreds of cancer patients. In April 2015, he announced the intention to invest INR 40–50 crores in online startups, expanding the YouWeCan proposition by setting up YouWeCan Ventures in order to do so.[130] In 2015, YouWeCan also initiated the nationwide cancer awareness in association with Jayakrishnan, the founder of Heyyo Media. The campaign took cancer awareness to many students across the country.[131] Yuvraj Singh also participated in the 'Celebrity Clásico 2016[132]' which was played with an objective to generate funds for charitable initiatives.

Cricket

Cricket is a bat-and-ball game played between two teams of eleven players on a field at the centre of which is a 22-yard (20-metre) pitch with a wicket at each end, each comprising two bails balanced on three stumps. The batting side scores runs by striking the ball bowled at the wicket with the bat (and running between the wickets), while the bowling and fielding side tries to prevent this (by preventing the ball from leaving the field, and getting the ball to either wicket) and dismiss each batter (so they are "out"). Means of dismissal include being bowled, when the ball hits the stumps and dislodges the bails, and by the fielding side either catchingthe ball after it is hit by the bat and before it hits the ground, or hitting a wicket with the ball before a batter can cross the creasein front of the wicket. When ten batters have been dismissed, the inningsends and the teams swap roles. The game is adjudicated by two umpires, aided by a third umpireand match refereein international matches. They communicate with two off-field scorerswho record the match's statistical information.

Forms of cricketrange from Twenty20, with each team batting for a single innings of 20 overs, to Test matchesplayed over five days. Traditionally cricketers play in all-white kit, but in limited overs cricketthey wear club or team colours. In addition to the basic kit, some players wear protective gearto prevent injury caused by the ball, which is a hard, solid spheroid made of compressed leatherwith a slightly raised sewn seam enclosing a corkcore layered with tightly wound string.

The earliest reference to cricket is in South East Englandin the mid-16th century. It spread globally with the expansion of the British Empire, with the first international matches in the second half of the 19th century. The game's governing body is the International Cricket Council(ICC), which has over 100 members, twelve of which are full memberswho play Test matches. The game's rules, the Laws of Cricket, are maintained by Marylebone Cricket Club(MCC) in London. The sport is followed primarily in the Indian subcontinent, Australasia, the United Kingdom, southern Africaand the West Indies.[1]Women's cricket, which is organised and played separately, has also achieved international standard. The most successful side playing international cricketis Australia, which has won seven One Day Internationaltrophies, including five World Cups, more than any other country and has been the top-rated Test sidemore than any other country.

History

Cricket is one of many games in the "club ball" sphere that basically involve hitting a ball with a hand-held implement; others include baseball(which shares many similaritieswith cricket, both belonging in the more specific bat-and-ball gamescategory[2]), golf, hockey, tennis, squash, badmintonand table tennis.[3]In cricket's case, a key difference is the existence of a solid target structure, the wicket (originally, it is thought, a "wicket gate" through which sheep were herded), that the batsman must defend.[4]The cricket historian Harry Althamidentified three "groups" of "club ball" games: the "hockey group", in which the ball is driven to and fro between two targets (the goals); the "golf group", in which the ball is driven towards an undefended target (the hole); and the "cricket group", in which "the ball is aimed at a mark (the wicket) and driven away from it".[5]

It is generally believed that cricket originated as a children's gamein the south-eastern counties of England, sometime during the medieval period.[4]Although there are claims for prior dates, the earliest definite reference to cricket being played comes from evidence given at a court case in Guildfordon Monday, 17 January 1597 (Julian calendar; equating to 30 January 1598 in the Gregorian calendar). The case concerned ownership of a certain plot of land and the court heard the testimony of a 59-year-old coroner, John Derrick, who gave witness that:[6][7][8]

Being a scholler in the ffree schoole of Guldefordhee and diverse of his fellows did runne and play there at creckett and other plaies.

Given Derrick's age, it was about half a century earlier when he was at school and so it is certain that cricket was being played c. 1550 by boys in Surrey.[8]The view that it was originally a children's game is reinforced by Randle Cotgrave's 1611 English-French dictionary in which he defined the noun "*crosse*" as "the crooked staff wherewith boys play at cricket" and the verb form "*crosser*" as "to play at cricket".[9][10]

One possible source for the sport's name is the Old Englishword "*cryce*" (or "*cricc*") meaning a crutch or staff. In Samuel Johnson's *Dictionary*, he derived cricket from "*cryce*, Saxon, a stick".[6]In Old French, the word "*criquet*" seems to have meant a kind of club or stick.[11]Given the strong medieval trade connections between south-east England and the County of Flanderswhen the latter belonged to the Duchy of Burgundy, the name may have been derived from the Middle Dutch(in use in Flandersat the time) "*krick*"(*-e*), meaning a stick (crook).[11]Another possible source is the Middle Dutch word "*krickstoel*", meaning a long low stool used for kneeling in church and which resembled the long low wicketwith two stumpsused in early cricket.[12]According to Heiner Gillmeister, a European language expert of Bonn University, "cricket" derives from the Middle Dutch phrase for hockey, *met de (krik ket)sen* (i.e., "with the stick chase").[13]Gillmeister has suggested that not only the name but also the sport itself may be of Flemish origin.[13]

Growth of amateur and professional cricket in England

Although the main object of the game has always been to score the most runs, the early form of cricket differed from the modern game in certain key technical aspects; the North American variant of cricket known as wicketretained many of these aspects.[14]The ballwas bowled underarmby the bowlerand along the ground towards a batsmanarmed with a batthat, in shape, resembled a hockey stick; the batsman defended a low, two-stump wicket; and runs were called notches because the scorersrecorded them by notching tally sticks.[15][16][17]

In 1611, the year Cotgrave's dictionary was published, ecclesiastical courtrecords at Sidleshamin Sussexstate that two parishioners, Bartholomew Wyatt and Richard Latter, failed to attend church on Easter Sunday because they were playing cricket. They were fined 12deach and ordered to do penance.[18]This is the earliest mention of adult participation in cricket and it was around the same time that the earliest known organised inter-parish or villagematch was played – at Chevening, Kent.[6][19]In 1624, a player called Jasper Vinalldied after he was accidentally struck on the head during a match between two parish teams in Sussex.[20]

Cricket remained a low-key local pursuit for much of the 17th century.[10]It is known, through numerous references found in the records of ecclesiastical court cases, to have been proscribed at times by the Puritansbefore and during the

Commonwealth.[21][22]The problem was nearly always the issue of Sunday play as the Puritans considered cricket to be "profane" if played on the Sabbath, especially if large crowds or gambling were involved. According to the social historian Derek Birley, there was a "great upsurge of sport after the Restoration" in 1660.[25]Gambling on sport became a problem significant enough for Parliament to pass the 1664 Gambling Act, limiting stakes to £100 which was, in any case, a colossal sum exceeding the annual income of 99% of the population.[25]Along with prizefighting, horse racing and blood sports, cricket was perceived to be a gambling sport.[26]Rich patrons made matches for high stakes, forming teams in which they engaged the first professional players.[27]By the end of the century, cricket had developed into a major sport that was spreading throughout England and was already being taken abroad by English mariners and colonisers – the earliest reference to cricket overseas is dated 1676.[28]A 1697 newspaper report survives of "a great cricket match" played in Sussex "for fifty guineas apiece" – this is the earliest known contest that is generally considered a First Class match.[29][30]

The patrons, and other players from the social class known as the "gentry", began to classify themselves as "amateurs"[fn 1] to establish a clear distinction from the professionals, who were invariably members of the working class, even to the point of having separate changing and dining facilities.[31]The gentry, including such high-ranking nobles as the Dukes of Richmond, exerted their honour code of noblesse oblige to claim rights of leadership in any sporting contests they took part in, especially as it was necessary for them to play alongside their "social inferiors" if they were to win their bets.[32]In time, a perception took hold that the typical amateur who played in first-class cricket, until 1962 when amateurism was abolished, was someone with a public school education who had then gone to one of Cambridge or Oxford University – society insisted that such people were "officers and gentlemen" whose destiny was to provide leadership.[33]In a purely financial sense, the cricketing amateur would theoretically claim expenses for playing while his professional counterpart played under contract and was paid a wage or match fee; in practice, many amateurs claimed more than actual expenditure and the derisive term "shamateur" was coined to describe the practice.[34][35]

English cricket in the 18th and 19th centuries

The game underwent major development in the 18th century to become England's national sport. Its success was underwritten by the twin necessities of patronage and betting.[36]Cricket was prominent in London as early as 1707 and, in the middle years of the century, large crowds flocked to matches on the Artillery Groundin FinsburyThe single wicketform of the sport attracted huge crowds and wagers to match, its popularity peaking in the 1748 season.[37]Bowling underwent an evolution around 1760 when bowlers began to pitch the ballinstead of rolling or skimming it towards the batsman. This caused a revolution in bat design because, to deal with the bouncing ball, it was necessary to introduce the modern straight bat in place of the old "hockey stick" shape. The Hambledon Clubwas founded in the 1760s and, for the next twenty years until the formation of Marylebone Cricket Club(MCC) and the opening of Lord's Old Groundin 1787, Hambledon was both the game's greatest club and its focal point.[citation needed]MCC quickly became the sport's premier club and the custodian of the Laws of Cricket. New Laws introduced in the latter part of the 18th century included the three stump wicket and leg before wicket(lbw).[39]

The 19th century saw underarm bowlingsuperseded by first roundarmand then overarm bowling. Both developments were controversial.[40]Organisation of the game at county level led to the creation of the county clubs, starting with Sussexin 1839.[41]In December 1889, the eight leading county clubs formed the official County Championship, which began in 1890.[42]

The most famous player of the 19th century was W. G. Grace, who started his long and influential career in 1865. It was especially during the career of Grace that the distinction between amateurs and professionals became blurred by the existence of players like him who were nominally amateur but, in terms of their financial gain, *de facto* professional. Grace himself was said to have been paid more money for playing cricket than any professional.[*citation needed*]

The last two decades before the First World War have been called the "Golden Age of cricket". It is a nostalgic name prompted by the collective sense of loss resulting from the war, but the period did produce some great players and memorable matches, especially as organised competition at county and Test level developed.[43]

Cricket becomes an international sport

Meanwhile, the British Empire had been instrumental in spreading the game overseas and by the middle of the 19th century it had become well established in Australia, the Caribbean, India, New Zealand, North America and South Africa.[44] In 1844, the first-ever international match took place between the United States and Canada.[45] In 1859, a team of English players went to North America on the first overseas tour.[46]

In 1862, an English team made the first tour of Australia.[47] The first Australian team to travel overseas consisted of Aboriginal stockmen who toured England in 1868.[48]

In 1876–77, an England team took part in what was retrospectively recognised as the first-ever Test match at the Melbourne Cricket Ground against Australia.[49] The rivalry between England and Australia gave birth to The Ashes in 1882, and this has remained Test cricket's most famous contest.[50] Test cricket began to expand in 1888–89 when South Africa played England.[*citation needed*]

World cricket in the 20th century

Don Bradman of Australia had a record Test batting average of 99.94.

The inter-war years were dominated by Australia's Don Bradman, statistically the greatest Test batsman of all time. Test cricket continued to expand during the 20th century with the addition of the West Indies (1928), New Zealand (1930) and India (1932) before the Second World War and then Pakistan (1952), Sri Lanka (1982), Zimbabwe (1992), Bangladesh (2000), Ireland and Afghanistan (both 2018) in the post-war period.[51][52]South Africawas banned from international cricket from 1970 to 1992 as part of the apartheid boycott.[53]

The rise of limited overs cricket

Cricket entered a new era in 1963 when English counties introduced the limited oversvariant.[54]As it was sure to produce a result, limited overs cricket was lucrative and the number of matches increased.[55]The first Limited Overs Internationalwas played in 1971 and the governing International Cricket Council(ICC), seeing its potential, staged the first limited overs Cricket World Cupin 1975.[56]In the 21st century, a new limited overs form, Twenty20, made an immediate impact.[citation needed]On 22 June 2017, Afghanistanand Irelandbecame the 11th and 12th ICC full members, enabling them to play Test cricket.[57][58]

Laws and gameplay

Main article: Laws of Cricket

In cricket, the rules of the game are specified in a code called *The Laws of Cricket*(hereinafter called "the Laws") which has a global remit. There are 42 Laws (always written with a capital "L"). The earliest known version of the code was drafted in 1744 and, since 1788, it has been owned and maintained by its custodian, the Marylebone Cricket Club(MCC) in London.[59]

Playing area

Main articles: Cricket field, Cricket pitch, Crease (cricket), and Wicket

Cricket is a bat-and-ball gameplayed on a cricket field(see image, right) between two teams of eleven players each.[60]The field is usually circular or oval in shape and the edge of the playing area is marked by a boundary, which may be a fence, part of the stands, a rope, a painted line or a combination of these; the boundary must if possible be marked along its entire length.[61]

In the approximate centre of the field is a rectangular pitch(see image, below) on which a wooden target called a wicketis sited at each end; the wickets are placed 22 yards (20 m) apart.[62]The pitch is a flat surface 10 feet (3.0 m) wide, with very short grass that tends to be worn away as the game progresses (cricket can also be played on artificial surfaces, notably matting). Each wicket is made of three wooden stumpstopped by two bails.[63]

As illustrated above, the pitch is marked at each end with four white painted lines: a bowling crease, a popping creaseand two return creases. The three stumps are aligned centrally on the bowling crease, which is eight feet eight inches long. The popping crease is drawn four feet in front of the bowling crease and parallel to it; although it is drawn as a twelve-foot line (six feet either side of the wicket), it is, in fact, unlimited in length. The return creases are drawn at right angles to the popping crease so that they intersect the ends of the bowling crease; each return crease is drawn as an eight-foot line, so that it extends four feet behind the bowling crease, but is also, in fact, unlimited in length.[64]

Match structure and closure

Main articles: Inningsand Result (cricket)

Before a match begins, the team captains(who are also players) toss a cointo decide which team will bat first and so take the first innings.[65]Inningsis the term used for each phase of play in the match.[65]In each innings, one team bats, attempting to scoreruns, while the other team bowlsand fieldsthe ball, attempting to restrict the scoring and dismissthe batsmen.[66][67]When the first innings ends, the teams change roles; there can be two to four innings depending upon the type of match. A match with four scheduled innings is played over three to five days; a match with two scheduled innings is usually completed in a single day.[65]During an innings, all eleven members of the fielding team take the field, but usually only two members of the batting team are on the field at any given time. The exception to this is if a batsman has any type of illness or injury restricting his or her ability to run, in this case the batsman is allowed a runner who can run between the wickets when the batsman hits a scoring run or runs,[68]though this does not apply in international cricket.[69]The order of batsmen is usually announced just before the match, but it can be varied.[60]

The main objective of each team is to score more runs than their opponents but, in some forms of cricket, it is also necessary to dismiss all of the opposition batsmen in their final innings in order to win the match, which would otherwise be drawn.[70] If the team batting last is all out having scored fewer runs than their opponents, they are said to have "lost by *n* runs" (where *n* is the difference between the aggregate number of runs scored by the teams). If the team that bats last scores enough runs to win, it is said to have "won by *n* wickets", where *n* is the number of wickets left to fall. For example, a team that passes its opponents' total having lost six wickets (i.e., six of their batsmen have been dismissed) have won the match "by four wickets".[70]

In a two-innings-a-side match, one team's combined first and second innings total may be less than the other side's first innings total. The team with the greater score is then said to have "won by an innings and *n* runs", and does not need to bat again: *n* is the difference between the two teams' aggregate scores. If the team batting last is all out, and both sides have scored the same number of runs, then the match is a tie; this result is quite rare in matches of two innings a side with only 62 happening in first-class matchesfrom the earliest known instance in 1741 until January 2017. In the traditional formof the game, if the time allotted for the match expires before either side can win, then the game is declared a draw.[70]

If the match has only a single innings per side, then a maximum number of oversapplies to each innings. Such a match is called a "limited overs" or "one-day" match, and the side scoring more runs wins regardless of the number of wickets lost, so that a draw cannot occur. If this kind of match is temporarily interrupted by bad weather, then a complex mathematical formula, known as the Duckworth–Lewis–Stern methodafter its developers, is often used to recalculate a new target score. A one-day match can also be declared a "no-result" if fewer than a previously agreed number of overs have been bowled by either team, in circumstances that make normal resumption of play impossible; for example, wet weather.[70]

In all forms of cricket, the umpires can abandon the match if bad light or rain makes it impossible to continue.[71] There have been instances of entire matches, even Test matches scheduled to be played over five days, being lost to bad weather without a ball being bowled: for example, the third Test of the 1970/71 series in Australia.[72]

Innings

Main article: Innings

The innings (ending with 's' in both singular and plural form) is the term used for each phase of play during a match. Depending on the type of match being played, each team has either one or two innings. Sometimes all eleven members of the batting side take a turn to bat but, for various reasons, an innings can end before they have all done so. The innings terminates if the batting team is "all out", a term defined by the Laws: "at the fall of a wicket or the retirement of a batsman, further balls remain to be bowled but no further batsman is available to come in".[65] In this situation, one of the batsmen has not been dismissed and is termed not out; this is because he has no partners left and there must always be two active batsmen while the innings is in progress.

An innings may end early while there are still two not out batsmen:[65]

- the batting team's captain may declare the innings closed even though some of his players have not had a turn to bat: this is a tactical decision by the captain, usually because he believes his team have scored sufficient runs and need time to dismiss the opposition in their innings
- the set number of overs (i.e., in a limited overs match) have been bowled
- the match has ended prematurely due to bad weather or running out of time
- in the final innings of the match, the batting side has reached its target and won the game.

Main article: Over (cricket)

The Laws state that, throughout an innings, "the ball shall be bowled from each end alternately in overs of 6 balls".[73] The name "over" came about because the umpire calls "Over!" when six balls have been bowled. At this point, another bowler is deployed at the other end, and the fielding side changes ends while the batsmen do not. A bowler cannot bowl two successive overs, although a bowler can (and usually does) bowl alternate overs, from the same end, for several overs which are termed a "spell". The batsmen do not change ends at the end of the over, and so the one who was non-striker is now the striker and vice versa. The umpires also change positions so that the one who was at "square leg" now stands behind the wicket at the non-striker's end and vice versa.[73]

Clothing and equipment

Main article: Cricket clothing and equipment

The wicket-keeper (a specialized fielder behind the batsman) and the batsmen wear protective gear because of the hardness of the ball, which can be delivered at speeds of more than 145 kilometres per hour (90 mph) and presents a major health and safety concern. Protective clothing includes pads(designed to protect the knees and shins), batting glovesor wicket-keeper's glovesfor the hands, a safety helmetfor the head and a boxfor male players inside the trousers (to protect the crotcharea).[74] Some batsmen wear additional padding inside their shirts and trousers such as thigh pads, arm pads, rib protectors and shoulder pads. The only fielders allowed to wear protective gear are those in positions very close to the batsman (i.e., if they are alongside or in front of him), but they cannot wear gloves or external leg guards.[75]

Subject to certain variations, on-field clothing generally includes a collared shirt with short or long sleeves; long trousers; woolen pullover (if needed); cricket cap(for fielding) or a safety helmet; and spiked shoes or boots to increase traction. The kit is traditionally all white and this remains the case in Test and first-class cricket but, in limited overs cricket, team colours are worn instead.[76]

Bat and ball

Main articles: Cricket bat and Cricket ball

The essence of the sport is that a bowlerdelivers(i.e., bowls) the ballfrom his or her end of the pitchtowards the batsmanwho, armed with a bat, is "on strike" at the other end (see next sub-section: *Basic gameplay*).

The batis made of wood, usually *salix alba*(white willow), and has the shape of a blade topped by a cylindrical handle. The blade must not be more than 4.25 inches (10.8 cm) wide and the total length of the bat not more than 38 inches (97 cm). There is no standard for the weight, which is usually between 2 lb 7 oz and 3 lb (1.1 and 1.4 kg).[77][78]

The ballis a hard leather-seamed spheroid, with a circumference of 9 inches (23 cm). The ball has a "seam": six rows of stitches attaching the leather shell of the ball to the string and cork interior. The seam on a new ball is prominent and helps the bowler propel it in a less predictable manner. During matches, the quality of the ball deteriorates to a point where it is no longer usable; during the course of this deterioration, its behaviour in flight will change and can influence the outcome of the match. Players will, therefore, attempt to modify the ball's behaviour by modifying its physical properties. Polishing the ball and wetting it with sweat or saliva is legal, even when the polishing is deliberately done on one side only to increase the ball's swing through the air, but the acts of rubbing other substances into the ball, scratching the surface or picking at the seam are illegal ball tampering.[79]

Player roles

Basic gameplay: bowler to batsman

During normal play, thirteen players and two umpiresare on the field. Two of the players are batsmen and the rest are all eleven members of the fielding team. The other nine players in the batting team are off the field in the pavilion. The image with overlay below shows what is happening when a ball is being bowled and which of the personnel are on or close to the pitch.[80]

In the photo, the two batsmen(3 & 8; wearing yellow) have taken position at each end of the pitch(6). Three members of the fieldingteam (4, 10 & 11; wearing dark blue) are in shot. One of the two umpires (1; wearing white hat) is stationed behind the wicket(2) at the bowler's(4) end of the pitch. The bowler (4) is bowlingthe ball(5) from his end of the pitch to the batsman (8) at the other end who is called the "striker". The other batsman (3) at the bowling end is called the "non-striker". The wicket-keeper(10), who is a specialist, is positioned behind the striker's wicket (9) and behind him stands one of the fielders in a position called "first slip" (11). While the bowler and the first slip are wearing conventional kit only, the two batsmen and the wicket-keeper are wearing protective gear including safety helmets, padded gloves and leg guards (pads).

While the umpire (1) in shot stands at the bowler's end of the pitch, his colleague stands in the outfield, usually in or near the fielding position called "square leg", so that he is in line with the popping crease(7) at the striker's end of the pitch. The bowling crease (not numbered) is the one on which the wicket is located between the return creases (12). The bowler (4) intends to hit the wicket (9) with the ball (5) or, at least, to prevent the striker (8) from scoring runs. The striker (8) intends, by using his bat, to defend his wicket and, if possible, to hit the ball away from the pitch in order to score runs.

Some players are skilled in both batting and bowling, or as either or these as well as wicket-keeping, so are termed all-rounders. Bowlers are classified according to their style, generally as fast bowlers, seam bowlersor spinners. Batsmen are classified according to whether they are right-handed or left-handed.

Fielding

Main article: Fielding (cricket)

Of the eleven fielders, three are in shot in the image above. The other eight are elsewhere on the field, their positions determined on a tactical basis by the captain or the bowler. Fielders often change position between deliveries, again as directed by the captain or bowler.[75]

If a fielder is injured or becomes ill during a match, a substitute is allowed to field instead of him, but the substitute cannot bowl or act as a captain, except in the case of concussion substitutes in international cricket.[69] The substitute leaves the field when the injured player is fit to return.[81] The Laws of Cricket were updated in 2017 to allow substitutes to act as wicket-keepers.[82]

Bowling and dismissal

Main articles: Bowling (cricket) and Dismissal (cricket)

Most bowlers are considered specialists in that they are selected for the team because of their skill as a bowler, although some are all-rounders and even specialist batsmen bowl occasionally. The specialists bowl several times during an innings but may not bowl two overs consecutively. If the captain wants a bowler to "change ends", another bowler must temporarily fill in so that the change is not immediate.[73]

A bowler reaches his delivery stride by means of a "run-up" and an over is deemed to have begun when the bowler starts his run-up for the first delivery of that over, the ball then being "in play".[73] Fast bowlers, needing momentum, take a lengthy run up while bowlers with a slow delivery take no more than a couple of steps before bowling. The fastest bowlers can deliver the ball at a speed of over 145 kilometres per hour (90 mph) and they sometimes rely on sheer speed to try to defeat the batsman, who is forced to react very quickly.[84] Other fast bowlers rely on a mixture of speed and guile by making the ball seam or swing (i.e. curve) in flight. This type of delivery can deceive a batsman into miscuing his shot, for example, so that the ball just touches the edge of the bat and can then be "caught behind" by the wicket-keeper or a slip fielder.[84] At the other end of the bowling scale is the spin bowler who bowls at a relatively slow pace and relies entirely on guile to deceive the batsman. A spinner will often "buy his wicket" by "tossing one up" (in a slower, steeper parabolic path) to lure the batsman into making a poor shot. The batsman has to be very wary of such deliveries as they are often "flighted" or spun so that the ball will not behave quite as he expects and he could be "trapped" into getting himself out.[85] In between the pacemen and the spinners are the medium paced seamers who rely on persistent accuracy to try to contain the rate of scoring and wear down the batsman's concentration.[84]

There are ten ways in which a batsman can be dismissed: five relatively common and five extremely rare. The common forms of dismissal are bowled,[86] caught,[87] leg before wicket(lbw),[88] run out[89] and stumped.[90] Rare methods are hit wicket,[91] hit the ball twice,[92] obstructing the field,[93] handled the ball[94] and timed out.[95] The Laws state that the fielding team, usually the bowler in practice, must appeal for a dismissal before the umpire can give his decision. If the batsman is out, the umpire raises a forefinger and says "Out!"; otherwise, he will shake his head and say "Not out".[96] There is, effectively, an eleventh method of dismissal, retired out, which is not an on-field dismissal as such but rather a retrospective one for which no fielder is credited.[97]

Batting, runs and extras

Main articles: Batting (cricket), Run (cricket), and Extra (cricket)

Batsmen take turns to bat via a batting order which is decided beforehand by the team captain and presented to the umpires, though the order remains flexible when the captain officially nominates the team.[60] Substitute batsmen are generally not allowed,[81] except in the case of concussion substitutes in international cricket.[69]

In order to begin batting the batsman first adopts a batting stance. Standardly, this involves adopting a slight crouch with the feet pointing across the front of the wicket, looking in the direction of the bowler, and holding the bat so it passes over the feet and so its tip can rest on the ground near to the toes of the back foot.[98]

A skilled batsman can use a wide array of "shots" or "strokes" in both defensive and attacking mode. The idea is to hit the ball to the best effect with the flat surface of the bat's blade. If the ball touches the side of the bat it is called an "edge". The batsman does not have to play a shot and can allow the ball to go through to the wicketkeeper. Equally, he does not have to attempt a run when he hits the ball with his bat. Batsmen do not always seek to hit the ball as hard as possible, and a good player can score runs just by making a deft stroke with a turn of the wrists or by simply "blocking" the ball but directing it away from fielders so that he has time to take a run. A wide variety of shots are played, the batsman's repertoire including strokes named according to the style of swing and the direction aimed: e.g., "cut", "drive", "hook", "pull".[99]

The batsman on strike (i.e. the "striker") must prevent the ball hitting the wicket, and try to score runs by hitting the ball with his bat so that he and his partner have time to run from one end of the pitch to the other before the fielding side can return the ball. To register a run, both runners must touch the ground behind the popping crease with either their bats or their bodies (the batsmen carry their bats as they run). Each completed run increments the score of both the team and the striker.[100]

The decision to attempt a run is ideally made by the batsman who has the better view of the ball's progress, and this is communicated by calling: usually "yes", "no" or "wait". More than one run can be scored from a single hit: hits worth one to three runs are common, but the size of the field is such that it is usually difficult to run four or more.[100] To compensate for this, hits that reach the boundary of the field are automatically awarded four runs if the ball touches the ground *en route* to the boundary or six runs if the ball clears the boundary without touching the ground within the boundary. In these cases the batsmen do not need to run.[101] Hits for five are unusual and generally rely on the help of "overthrows" by a fielder returning the ball. If an odd number of runs is scored by the striker, the two batsmen have changed ends, and the one who was non-striker is now the striker. Only the striker can score individual runs, but all runs are added to the team's total.[100]

Additional runs can be gained by the batting team as extras (called "sundries" in Australia) due to errors made by the fielding side. This is achieved in four ways: no-ball, a penalty of one extra conceded by the bowler if he breaks the rules;[102] wide, a penalty of one extra conceded by the bowler if he bowls so that the ball is out of the batsman's reach;[103]bye, an extra awarded if the batsman misses the ball and it goes past the wicket-keeper and gives the batsmen time to run in the conventional way;[104]leg bye, as for a bye except that the ball has hit the batsman's body, though not his bat.[104]If the bowler has conceded a no-ball or a wide, his team incurs an additional penalty because that ball (i.e., delivery) has to be bowled again and hence the batting side has the opportunity to score more runs from this extra ball.[102][103]

Specialist roles

Main articles: Captain (cricket) and Wicket-keeper

The captain is often the most experienced player in the team, certainly the most tactically astute, and can possess any of the main skillsets as a batsman, a bowler or a wicket-keeper. Within the Laws, the captain has certain responsibilities in terms of nominating his players to the umpires before the match and ensuring that his players conduct themselves "within the spirit and traditions of the game as well as within the Laws".[60]

The wicket-keeper (sometimes called simply the "keeper") is a specialist fielder subject to various rules within the Laws about his equipment and demeanour. He is the only member of the fielding side who can effect a stumping and is the only one permitted to wear gloves and external leg guards.[105] Depending on their primary skills, the other ten players in the team tend to be classified as specialist batsmen or specialist bowlers. Generally, a team will include five or six specialist batsmen and four or five specialist bowlers, plus the wicket-keeper.[106][107]

Umpires and scorers

Main articles: Umpire (cricket), Scoring (cricket), and Cricket statistics

The game on the field is regulated by the two umpires, one of whom stands behind the wicket at the bowler's end, the other in a position called "square leg" which is about 15–20 metres away from the batsman on strike and in line with the popping crease on which he is taking guard. The umpires have several responsibilities including adjudication on whether a ball has been correctly bowled (i.e., not a no-ball or a wide); when a run is scored; whether a batsman is out (the fielding side must first appeal to the umpire, usually with the phrase "How's that?" or "Owzat?"); when intervals start and end; and the suitability of the pitch, field and weather for playing the game. The umpires are authorised to interrupt or even abandon a match due to circumstances likely to endanger the players, such as a damp pitch or deterioration of the light.[71]

Off the field in televised matches, there is usually a third umpire who can make decisions on certain incidents with the aid of video evidence. The third umpire is mandatory under the playing conditions for Test and Limited Overs International matches played between two ICC full member countries. These matches also have a match referee whose job is to ensure that play is within the Laws and the spirit of the game.[71]

The match details, including runs and dismissals, are recorded by two official scorers, one representing each team. The scorers are directed by the hand signals of an umpire (see image, right). For example, the umpire raises a forefinger to signal that the batsman is out (has been dismissed); he raises both arms above his head if the batsman has hit the ball for six runs. The scorers are required by the Laws to record all runs scored, wickets taken and overs bowled; in practice, they also note significant amounts of additional data relating to the game.[108]

A match's statistics are summarised on a scorecard. Prior to the popularisation of scorecards, most scoring was done by men sitting on vantage points cuttings notches on tally sticks and runs were originally called notches.[109] According to Rowland Bowen, the earliest known scorecard templates were introduced in 1776 by T. Pratt of Sevenoaks and soon came into general use.[110] It is believed that scorecards were printed and sold at Lord's for the first time in 1846.[111]

Spirit of the Game
Main article: Laws of Cricket

Besides observing the Laws, cricketers must respect the "Spirit of Cricket," which is the "Preamble to the Laws," first published in the 2000 code, and updated in 2017, and now opens with this statement:[112]

"Cricket owes much of its appeal and enjoyment to the fact that it should be played not only according to the Laws, but also within the Spirit of Cricket".

The Preamble is a short statement that emphasises the "Positive behaviours that make cricket an exciting game that encourages leadership, friendship, and teamwork."[113]

The major responsibility for ensuring fair play is placed firmly on the captains, but extends to all players, umpires, teachers, coaches, and parents involved.

The umpires are the sole judges of fair and unfair play. They are required under the Laws to intervene in case of dangerous or unfair play or in cases of unacceptable conduct by a player.

Previous versions of the Spirit identified actions that were deemed contrary (for example, appealing knowing that the batsman is not out) but all specifics are now covered in the Laws of Cricket, the relevant governing playing regulations and disciplinary codes, or left to the judgement of the umpires, captains, their clubs and governing bodies. The terse expression of the Spirit of Cricket now avoids the diversity of cultural conventions that exist in the detail of sportsmanship – or its absence.

Women's cricket

Women's cricket was first recorded in Surrey in 1745.[114] International development began at the start of the 20th century and the first Test Match was played between Australia and England in December 1934.[115] The following year, New Zealand women joined them, and in 2007 Netherlands women became the tenth women's Test nation when they made their debut against South Africa women. In 1958, the International Women's Cricket Council was founded (it merged with the ICC in 2005).[115] In 1973, the first Cricket World Cup of any kind took place when a Women's World Cup was held in England.[115] In 2005, the International Women's Cricket Council was merged with the International Cricket Council (ICC) to form one unified body to help manage and develop cricket. The ICC Women's Rankings were launched on 1 October 2015 covering all three formats of women's cricket. In October 2018 following the ICC's decision to award T20 International status to all members, the Women's rankings were split into separate ODI(for Full Members) and T20I lists.[116]

Governance

The International Cricket Council(ICC), which has its headquarters in Dubai, is the global governing body of cricket. It was founded as the Imperial Cricket Conference in 1909 by representatives from England, Australia and South Africa, renamed the International Cricket Conference in 1965 and took up its current name in 1989.[115]The ICC in 2017 has 105 member nations, twelve of which hold full membership and can play Test cricket.[117]The ICC is responsible for the organisation and governance of cricket's major international tournaments, notably the men's and women's versions of the Cricket World Cup. It also appoints the umpires and referees that officiate at all sanctioned Test matches, Limited Overs Internationals and Twenty20 Internationals.

Each member nation has a national cricket board which regulates cricket matches played in its country, selects the national squad, and organises home and away tours for the national team.[118]In the West Indies, which for cricket purposes is a federation of nations, these matters are addressed by Cricket West Indies.[119]

The table below lists the ICC full members and their national cricket boards:[120]

Types of match

Cricket is a multi-faceted sport with multiple formats that can effectively be divided into first-class cricket, limited overs cricketand, historically, single wicket cricket. The highest standard is Test cricket(always written with a capital "T") which is in effect the international version of first-class cricket and is restricted to teams representing the twelve countries that are full members of the ICC (see above). Although the term "Test match" was not coined until much later, Test cricket is deemed to have begun with two matches between Australiaand Englandin the 1876-77 Australian season; since 1882, most Test series between England and Australia have been played for a trophy known as The Ashes. The term "first-class", in general usage, is applied to top-level domestic cricket. Test matches are played over five days and first-class over three to four days; in all of these matches, the teams are allotted two innings each and the draw is a valid result.[122]

Limited overs cricket is always scheduled for completion in a single day, and the teams are allotted one innings each. There are two types: List Awhich normally allows fifty overs per team; and Twenty20in which the teams have twenty overs each. Both of the limited overs forms are played internationally as Limited Overs Internationals(LOI) and Twenty20 Internationals(T20I). List A was introduced in England in the 1963 season as a knockout cup contested by the first-class county clubs. In 1969, a national league competition was established. The concept was gradually introduced to the other leading cricket countries and the first limited overs international was played in 1971. In 1975, the first Cricket World Cuptook place in England. Twenty20 is a new variant of limited overs itself with the purpose being to complete the match within about three hours, usually in an evening session. The first Twenty20 World Championshipwas held in 2007. Limited overs matches cannot be drawn, although a tie is possible and an unfinished match is a "no result".[123][124]

Single wicket was popular in the 18th and 19th centuries and its matches were generally considered **top-class. In this form, although each team may have**from one to six players, there is only one batsman in at a time and he must face every delivery bowled while his innings lasts. Single wicket has rarely been played since limited overs cricket began. Matches tended to have two innings per team like a full first-class one and they could end in a draw.[125]

Competitions

Cricket is played at both the international and domestic level. There is one major international championship per format, and top-level domestic competitions mirror the three main international formats. There are now a number of T20 leagues, which have spawned a "T20 freelancer" phenomenon.[126]

International competitions

Main article: International cricket

Most international matches are played as parts of 'tours', when one nation travels to another for a number of weeks or months, and plays a number of matches of various sorts against the host nation. Sometimes a perpetual trophyis awarded to the winner of the Test series, the most famous of which is The Ashes.

The ICC also organises competitions that are for several countries at once, including the Cricket World Cup, ICC T20 World Cupand ICC Champions Trophy. A league competition for Test matches played as part of normal tours, the ICC World Test Championship, had been proposed several times, and its first instancebegan in 2019. A league competition for ODIs, the ICC Cricket World Cup Super League, began in August 2020. The ICC maintains Test rankings, ODI rankingsand T20 rankingssystems for the countries which play these forms of cricket.

Competitions for member nations of the ICC with Associate statusinclude the ICC Intercontinental Cup, for first-class cricket matches, and the World Cricket Leaguefor one-day matches, the final matches of which now also serve as the ICC World Cup Qualifier.

National competitions

See also: Category:Domestic cricket competitions

First-class cricket in England is played for the most part by the 18 county clubs which contest the County Championship. The concept of a champion countyhas existed since the 18th century but the official competition was not established until 1890.[42]The most successful club has been Yorkshire, who had won 32 official titles (plus one shared) as of 2019.[127]

Australia established its national first-class championship in 1892–93 when the Sheffield Shieldwas introduced. In Australia, the first-class teams represent the various states.[128]New South

Waleshas the highest number of titles.

The other ICC full members have national championship trophies called the Ahmad Shah Abdali 4-day Tournament(Afghanistan); the National Cricket League(Bangladesh); the Ranji Trophy(India); the Inter-Provincial Championship(Ireland); the Plunket Shield(New Zealand); the Quaid-e-Azam Trophy(Pakistan); the Currie Cup(South Africa); the Premier Trophy(Sri Lanka); the Shell Shield(West Indies); and the Logan Cup(Zimbabwe).

Club and school cricket

Main articles: Village cricket, Club cricket, and Schools cricket

The world's earliest known cricket match was a village cricketmeeting in Kentwhich has been deduced from a 1640 court case recording a "cricketing" of "the Weald and the Upland" versus "the Chalk Hill" at Chevening"about thirty years since" (i.e., c. 1611). Inter-parish contests became popular in the first half of the 17th century and continued to develop through the 18th with the first local leagues being founded in the second half of the 19th.[19]

At the grassroots level, local club cricketis essentially an amateur pastime for those involved but still usually involves teams playing in competitions at weekends or in the evening. Schools cricket, first known in southern England in the 17th century, has a similar scenario and both are widely played in the countries where cricket is popular.[129]Although there can be variations in game format, compared with professional cricket, the Laws are always observed and club/school matches are therefore formal and competitive events.[130]The sport has numerous informal variants such as French cricket.[131]

Culture

Influence on everyday life

Cricket has had a broad impact on popular culture, both in the Commonwealth of Nationsand elsewhere. It has, for example, influenced the lexicon of these nations, especially the English language, with various phrases such as "that's not cricket" (that's unfair), "had a good innings" (lived a long life) and "sticky wicket".

"On a sticky wicket" (*aka* "sticky dog" or "glue pot")[132]is a metaphor[133]used to describe a difficult circumstance. It originated as a term for difficult batting conditions in cricket, caused by a damp and soft pitch.[134]

In the arts and popular culture

See also: *Cricket in fiction, Cricket in film and television,* and *Cricket poetry*

Cricket is the subject of works by noted English poets, including William Blakeand Lord Byron.[135]*Beyond a Boundary*(1963), written by Trinidadian C. L. R. James, is often named the best book on any sport ever written.[136]

In the visual arts, notable cricket paintings include Albert Chevallier Tayler's *Kent vs Lancashire at Canterbury*(1907) and Russell Drysdale's *The Cricketers*(1948), which has been called "possibly the most famous Australian painting of the 20th century." French impressionistCamille Pissarropainted cricket on a visit to England in the 1890s. Francis Bacon, an avid cricket fan, captured a batsman in motion.Caribbeanartist Wendy Nanan's cricket images are featured in a limited edition first day cover for Royal Mail's "World of Invention" stamp issue, which celebrated the London Cricket Conference 1–3 March 2007, first international workshop of its kind and part of the celebrations leading up to the 2007 Cricket World Cup.

Influence on other sports

Cricket has close historical ties with Australian rules footballand many players have competed at top levels in both sports. In 1858, prominent Australian cricketer Tom Willscalled for the formation of a "foot-ball club" with "a code of laws" to keep cricketers fit during the off-season. The Melbourne Football Clubwas founded the following year, and Wills and three other members codified the first laws of the game. It is typically played on modified cricket fields.

In England, a number of association footballclubs owe their origins to cricketers who sought to play football as a means of keeping fit during the winter months. Derby Countywas founded as a branch of the Derbyshire County Cricket Club in 1884; Aston Villa(1874) and Everton(1876) were both founded by members of church cricket teams.Sheffield United's Bramall Laneground was, from 1854, the home of the Sheffield Cricket Club, and then of Yorkshire; it was not used for football until 1862 and was shared by Yorkshire and Sheffield United from 1889 to 1973.

In the late 19th century, a former cricketer, English-born Henry Chadwickof Brooklyn, New York, was credited with devising the baseball box score(which he adapted from the cricket scorecard) for reporting game events. The first box score appeared in an 1859 issue of the *Clipper*.The statistical record is so central to the game's "historical essence" that Chadwick is sometimes referred to as "the Father of Baseball" because he facilitated the popularity of the sport in its early days.

www.ingramcontent.com/pod-product-compliance
Lightning Source LLC
LaVergne TN
LVHW041548060526
838200LV00037B/1192